FROM THE DEPTHS OF MY SOUL

SEARCHING FOR THE

LOVE

OF JESUS CHRIST

KIMBERLY CHERIE BRANCH

Published by Victorious You Press™
Charlotte NC, USA

TITLE: FROM THE DEPTHS OF MY SOUL
First Printed: 2024
Cover Designer: KellyVision
Editor: Angela McClain
ISBN: 978-1-959719-37-3

Printed in the United States of America

For details email joan@victoriousyoupress.com
or visit us at www.victoriousyoupress.com

DEDICATION

TO MY DAUGHTERS

You have come along with me on this journey and sometimes you didn't agree with my choices. However, as obedient children, you followed your mom. Now that I have rededicated my life to our Savior, Jesus Christ, my prayer is that you will continue to follow your mom as I follow Christ.

TO MY MOTHER

I could not have become who I am without you. Thank you for allowing me to share a part of your story, and thank you for loving and supporting my every desire.

CONTENTS

INTRODUCTION

A few nights before I began writing this book, I was aroused from a dream. As I drifted out of this dream state, I made a mental note of the images I had seen. Then I asked, "Holy Spirit, what do you want me to remember from that dream?"

One thing I remembered from the dream that stood out was the image of floors. Floors? "What are you trying to tell me?" I asked. I heard the Holy Spirit answer, "Foundations."

If you are asking *"How did you hear Him? Was it a sound in your ear like when a person speaks to you?"* Yes. The voice of the Holy Spirit sounds like a person speaking. It is a still, yet profound knowing that resonates as a weighty thought, so when He speaks, I have a sense that what I hear is an absolute and definitive truth. That's what makes it so profound whenever He speaks.

Prior to having that dream, I was prepared to share the different experiences I've had along my spiritual journey. As I sat poised to write, I could not reconcile how sharing would help build up the kingdom of God.

What the Holy Spirit revealed was my life experiences. Insight and enlightenment shared in this book would serve as the foundation to demonstrate how much Jesus loves us--no matter how far from the mark we feel we have fallen. The sovereign God, the All-Knowing One, gave me the clarity I needed to begin writing this book.

Have you ever felt lost in life, abandoned, or unseen? Have you ever felt neglected, abused, or without hope? I have good news for those who have felt dirty or unworthy of love. There is absolutely NOTHING that can separate you from the love of Christ. The burden you have been carrying will be lifted as I share my journey from Mormon, to witchcraft, and back to Christ.

My story is a testimony of how much Jesus loves us. Even when we turn away from Him, His outstretched arms are always ready to embrace us. Love, grace, and mercy are always extended, giving us an opportunity, at any given time, to come, rest, and lay down our burdens.

John 15:13 makes it clear that there is no greater love than the love that Jesus has for us. Not only did Jesus die for us, but He calls us "friends."

So, friend, whether you are reading this book, listening to it on audio, or taking an online course, please know that God sees you and He cares so much for you. He wants YOU to have hope, which is the foundation of this book. At the end of each chapter, you will find Scriptures to guide you in your journey. Applying God's Word to every issue you face in life is transforming and liberating.

* * *

LET US PRAY

Lord God in Heaven, my Father, my Provider, my Way Maker, my Peace, my Banner, my Warrior, and the Lover of my Soul; I thank You for allowing me to share my experiences in this book with the sole purpose of lifting You up so that You can draw men unto You.

I thank You for trusting me with this assignment and giving me an opportunity to do kingdom work. Thank You, Holy Spirit, my advocate, for apart from You I can do nothing; but through the strength that Jesus Christ gives me, I can do all the things You have commissioned me to do. I thank You for the love that You have poured out so lavishly upon me, and I thank You for all who have shared time and space with me on this journey. I thank You for my ups and my downs. Father, I come with just one request--that the heart of the person reading this book be drawn into a deeper and intimate relationship with You. If they don't know You as their Savior, I pray they have a radical encounter with You to renew their mind and transform their lives in an instant.

Lord, Your Word is true, and will accomplish whatever You send to do in the lives of each reader. As I share my journey, I put my complete trust this story will accomplish Your desire to manifest in the life of every reader. I thank You and I consider it already done in the matchless name of Jesus. Amen.

* * *

Ask and it will be given to you; seek and you will find; knock and the door will be opened to you. For everyone who asks receives; the one who seeks finds; and to the one who knocks, the door will be opened. Matthew 7:7-8 (NIV)

I AM DONE!

"*I AM DONE with searching for happiness in all the wrong places and I AM DONE with Mormons! I AM DONE with orishas, crystals, spells, and candles! I AM DONE with the gods I made out of men, and done with the gods who promised equality with Elohim. In this empty darkness I find myself in, I am tired and have nothing more to give. I AM DONE wearing a smile that hides my pain. I AM DONE holding on to secrets and pain forced on me by others. I AM DONE hoping that someone will see the suffering in my eyes, and I AM DONE waiting for someone to acknowledge me (beyond my circumstances). I AM DONE with loneliness and abandonment. I AM DONE with me, my decisions, and my actions. I AM DONE playing GOD!!"*

Yup! I had reached that place in my life, and I had nothing else to give. How did I get there? Let's start where everything starts—the beginning.

In my humble beginnings, I lived a perfect life, in a very nice house, with both of my parents. My mom worked for a major finance company, and always owned her own car. My favorite was the burgundy and white Chrysler that my mom named Steve. Whenever my family members needed help, whether they needed a ride, a place to live, or Christmas toys for the kids, my mom was the go-to person. She was my hero and I loved everything about her.

She was always busy helping others. No matter how busy she was--she always made special time for me. I enjoyed when she took me shopping or spent time playing games with me. In my eyes, my mom was perfect, and I admired so much about her. From her light, smooth skin, to her eyes that seemed to sparkle when she smiled, to her white, straight teeth which were the perfect accent for her full cheeks.

My mom had a classic style I loved. Her wardrobe consisted of skirt suits with collared blazers and shirts, and cardigan sweaters with argyle prints. I even incorporated that argyle print into my wardrobe with the socks I wore. I loved playing in my mom's shoes (the heels were so high). My favorite pair were her blue heels with the ankle strap and the blue leather band that went across the toes. They were the only pair of her heeled shoes I could walk in. I called them the Herman Munster shoes, because the heels were chunky.

Intelligent and multi-talented, my mom had a keen understanding of finances. Her boss, a savvy Jewish businessman, pulled her aside one day and said, "Mary, I'm going to teach you how to prepare income taxes so that you will always have a way to provide for you and your daughter." My mom learned well, and, in fact, she taught me how to prepare taxes. A natural-born entrepreneur, my mom would form a team (my Aunt Lillie and a few others) and cook greens, minced barbecue, macaroni and cheese, fried fish, and baked cakes to sell to friends and family. She always found a way to make money, and I learned my hustle from watching her.

As amazing as my mom was, she fell in love with a man who took her down a path that was unfamiliar, unforgiving, and full of darkness. My mom was the breadwinner of the family, and I knew my dad had girlfriends, so when he moved out, I imagine my mom had reached the point where something had to give. That was the point when my life changed from being a happy kid living with both of my parents, to a life of chaos. I saw the pain and struggle my mom endured, and my heart was heavy for her.

For most of my teenage years, I witnessed my mom's battle with drug addiction and her many failed attempts at rehab. We are often affected by the wounds of our childhood; those secret things which aren't usually mentioned, but hang like a weight around the neck. I believe the drugs made it easier for her to carry the weight of her secrets.

I kept my mom in prayer, called out her name daily before the throne of grace, and I "covered her with the blood of Jesus." I didn't understand what that meant, but I knew it was done in church, so I did it for my mom. I was concerned about what the drugs would do to her, I was also concerned for her physical safety. I'd witnessed how drug dealers with a new batch of drugs would give out free samples by tossing them in the air and watching while people were scrambling on the ground for them. I didn't want my mom to get hurt in the chaos, so I did what I could—prayed. I wasn't very familiar with the Bible back then, but I had faith that God would deliver her. In the meantime, life pressed in.

I noticed a change in my mom's behavior. She was talking on the phone more than usual; she was always tired, and she started hanging out more with her friends, going places I could not go. When her friends came over, they stayed up late at night and started gathering in the bedroom behind closed doors. *What is that smell?* Smoke rings hung in the air, and it stank! There were nights when I was home alone and called around to family looking for her. She didn't like that because she was never with family, but I didn't know who else to call. One evening, I came home and found her balled up in the chair in the living room, moaning and crying. I had never seen her like that, and I was scared. Her face didn't look the same. Her beautiful smile was gone, and the light that once danced in her eyes was replaced with a look of pain. The next thing I knew, we were moving.

These guys came to the house and put all our stuff in black trash bags and set them out on the sidewalk. My mom seemed to be preoccupied with something else, so I helped the men—I thought I was supposed to. From there, we moved from house to house, and each one was worse than the one before it. There was less food, less of my mom, but more of that awful familiar smell. My TV, my VCR, and my Betamax had disappeared. No more nice home with custom upholstered furniture or anything that resembled my previously perfect life.

Occasionally, my mom gave me money to go to the supermarket, which was down the street from where we lived. She let me buy whatever I wanted, so I'd buy snacks, juices, pencils, or thumbtacks. During a time when my life was being shaped by a broken home with one parent addicted to drugs; I clung to my adolescence by buying thumbtacks and pencils. At one point, the only thing in our fridge was an open can of pork and beans. I hated pork and beans! My grandmother's sister (Aunt Lillie) had bought me an old cosmetic case that she found at a thrift store. It was blue and about 14x8x8 with a brass closure on the front that flipped open when the lock was pushed. It was perfect for the peanut butter, jelly, and bread that she told me to keep in my case (in the event I got hungry). My Aunt Lillie looked out for me and made sure I knew I could always come to her house for something to eat. I occasionally walked to her house late at night, or as soon as the sun came up just to get something to eat, and when I did, I felt ashamed. People saw I had no food, no mom who cared, no stable home, and I thought my situation defined me. Seeds of unworthiness took root in my heart, and every day I felt like something was wrong with me. It had to be. I felt alone in the nightmare I was going through and wanted to hide from the world. I couldn't physically hide, but I hid by conforming to what I thought people expected of me. I held people at a distance, or I overextended myself. It was my way of keeping the abandoned, hungry little girl hidden.

Soon after I finished high school, I had a daughter of my own. Her dad, Kevin, was someone I had loved for as long as I could remember. Our moms were best friends from their childhood and our families were always together. We'd go shopping, I spent the night at their house, and we basically shared life together.

Kevin was thin, dark-skinned and had more confidence than any one person should have. When he spoke, it was authoritative, commanding, and in control. Once I reached adulthood and realized he wasn't "really" my cousin, I decided I wanted to be with him. I had known him for years and I trusted him. I didn't think he would hurt me by leaving the way my dad did. I didn't think he would tear me apart like my mom's friend did her. That's what I told myself as I looked to him for the love and security that was absent from my life.

Kevin lived with his mom and slept in the basement. I had been staying with him and his family because I had a sense of security there. His aunts cooked dinner every day and the gas and electricity were never turned off.

One night the basement where Kevin and I were sleeping flooded! There was water everywhere, and I was frantic! I didn't know where I was going to go, but I didn't want to leave his side.

"What are we going to do?" I asked. He didn't seem worried, but I was. I didn't want to go back to my mom's house. I slumped down in the corner of the couch, trying to figure out where I was going to go. Kevin's mom and aunts were talking about what caused the basement to flood and how they were going to fix it. I was in the same room with them, but their conversation sounded like muffled chatter in the distance. I was rehearsing in my mind a way to ask if I could stay there and sleep on the couch.

In the meantime, Kevin was downstairs in the basement. When he called me to come down there, I slowly walked down the basement stairs and when I got to the bottom step, I saw that he had used boards to create a path for me to walk from the last dry step to the bed. Holding my hand, he guided me along the short walk to the bed, then he dried my feet with a towel.

The next night, Kevin's friend, who lived down the street, delivered a message to me.

"Kevin said 'come here, " his friend told me.

"Where is he?" I asked.

"He's at my house and he wants you to come down there."

I walked down the street to his friend's house and when I walked in the front door, it was dark inside. Finding my way upstairs and down a long hallway toward the bedroom, I found Kevin waiting for me in the bathroom. He had run a bubble bath for me, and let me tell you, at that moment, I was *all* his.

A few weeks later, he started telling me to go stay at my mom's house. At first, I didn't understand why, but his cousins couldn't keep his secret—he was still seeing other women. When I found that out, I threw all his clothes on the bed...the bed I thought was ours...the bed where he took the best parts of me...the bed where he hurt me. I lit a match, held it while, thinking: *Should I do it? I loved him and did whatever he told me to do. I gave him whatever he wanted!* I took a deep breath in. The rest is between me and my Savior.

After that episode, I reluctantly went back to live with my mom. My daughter was just a few months old, and during the summer when our gas and electricity were turned off, it was too hot to sleep in our room. I made a palette on the living room floor and left the front door open to catch a breeze. One of the older guys from the neighborhood offered to sit on the steps to stand guard and made sure no one bothered us. On another occasion (we had moved again) it was in the dead of winter, and we were once again without electricity. To keep my child warm, I pulled a recliner close to the stove and we slept in front of it with the oven door open. That life was not the life I wanted for me and my daughter, and I decided that I had to make sure my daughter was warm, had a place to rest her head, and food to eat. I was determined to save her, and in doing so, I was hoping to save myself.

One of my mom's drug friends had been suggesting I would do well if I started working at the strip club where she was working. She told me I had a cute butt and that with my red glasses (that everyone else made fun of), the men would love me. At the time, I had no food, no gas, no electricity, and the rent was months behind, so I figured I would do what I had to do. When I was ready, I walked down to one of the more upscale strip clubs, presented myself to the bartender, and I was hired. He liked my red glasses.

Most days, I sat and prayed that none of the men at the club would speak to me, and for the most part they didn't. I was naïve and had no idea about what to do. I worked the day shift, so by the time most of the debauchery started, my shift was ending. I learned a little bit about my co-workers. One of the girls was a nurse paying off student loans, and another was a homemaker who was living a double life. Some were there because their pimp made them come and even sat in the bar with them. I made sure not to smile too much in their direction, because I didn't want to give anybody the opportunity to approach me.

A few of the other girls offered me tips on how to not get caught up in the life, and I was eager to learn from them.

"Just make your money and go home alone," one of them advised.

I already knew from my Aunt Lillie to never leave my drink unattended, but I could use all the advice I could get.

Another co-worker advised me to let the bartender know (at the beginning of my shift) that if anybody buys me a drink, to give me only soda. I paid attention to their advice, and I was a good student. Once I invited a friend to come hang out and she was so excited and proud of my pole abilities. "That's my friend!" she said excitedly while clapping her hands. The ladies had taught me that too.

Just like my mom, I could recognize an opportunity and monetize it. I took the money I made from that job and flipped it into a business. I hired a few ladies and took them out to do parties, which paid very well! It wasn't long before I was finally able to move out of my mom's house and into my own apartment. I re-enrolled at the community college and was studying to get a degree in accounting. While I was working and at school, my mom was taking care of my daughter.

When I met Jasper, I was still working at the strip club. He used to stop by my mom's house to check on things and made sure my daughter had food to eat. One time I questioned him about why he would buy a two-year-old a Big Mac! I could tell he was kind, I trusted him, and my daughter had become attached to him. One day, he told me that if I wanted to give up my job as a dancer, he would help me out financially. I stopped dancing, and he kept his word. A year later, our daughter was born.

My life had taken a turn for the better. I had moved across the street from the church I grew up in and when the memories of the time I spent there resurfaced, I started attending again. With the adult business behind me, I was taking steps toward a more wholesome life, and Jasper was spending more time at home and less time in the streets. One day we were talking on the phone, and he mentioned that he and his friend were walking to the store. I called him later to tell him about a job I had gotten, and he didn't answer. I waited for a few minutes and called him back again—still no answer. I could feel a sense of uneasiness because he *ALWAYS* answered my calls. Something was wrong.

When my phone finally rang, it was Jasper's grandmother calling to let me know that he and his friend were in the hospital. They had been shot! I literally ran to the hospital as fast as I could and when I got there, both families were already assembled in one room. The doctor explained that Jasper was in surgery and was expected to recover. Right then, a nurse whispered in the doctor's ear and the doctor immediately corrected her statement.

"I am so sorry, I apologize. Jasper was shot in the arm, the bullet traveled through his chest and exploded in his heart. There was nothing they could do."

It seemed as though time stood still. My heart stopped and I heard myself scream "Noooooo!" as I fell to my knees. All I could do was call on the name of Jesus.

I couldn't believe it. Not him! Not the one I felt safe with. Not the one who cared for me and both of my girls. Not the one who loved and accepted me unconditionally— the stripper me, the hungry me, the daughter of a drug addict me.

Was it my fault? *Maybe God took him as punishment.* The accusatory thoughts began. *Something is wrong with you,* I told myself as memories of the times when I decided to stay in bed with him instead of going to church. I was angry with myself. *Did I love him too much? Did God take him because I would rather spend a few more minutes at his side instead of doing anything else?* I wasn't mad at God, but I felt so ashamed. I felt guilty. I didn't know how to process those thoughts, feelings, and accusations, so I shut them up in a box in my mind and closed the door.

✳   ✳   ✳

Scriptures to use when dealing with shame

For if you forgive other people when they sin against you, your heavenly Father will also forgive you. Matthew 6:14 (NIV)

✳

I trust in you; do not let me be put to shame, nor let my enemies triumph over me. Psalm 25:2 (NIV)

✳

Do not be afraid; you will not be put to shame. Do not fear disgrace; you will not be humiliated. You will forget the shame of your youth and remember no more the reproach of your widowhood. Isaiah 54:4 (NIV)

Chapter 2
THE MORE

J asper loved the girls and did his best to provide for us. Even though the girls were young (eight months and three years old) I'm sure his absence hurt them as much as it hurt me. In my devastation, I turned back to the church. One day after service, I was feeling like there had to be more to my Christian walk than what I was experiencing. I felt empty, but I knew there was more to God—there had to be!

Reflecting on an encounter I had as a child while sitting in the sanctuary listening to the preacher deliver his message, as he was speaking, I felt the encapsulating love of God embracing me. I felt seen, and I had never felt so much love and tenderness before. My cousin kept asking me what was wrong, but I couldn't articulate what I was feeling, all I could do was weep. My cousin thought something was seriously wrong with me, and ran to get my Aunt Lillie. My aunt took one look at me and said, "She's okay. She's just feeling the Spirit."

What I experienced as that eight-year-old little girl sitting in the pew of that sanctuary was the "more" that I longed to experience again. I felt that there was some type of mystery that I wasn't privy to anymore. I felt that there were others who were having an experience with God that I wanted also. My soul and my spirit were craving a more intimate relationship with the Father, similar to what I experienced as a child. As I walked those few short steps from the church to home, I poured out my heart to God.

"Lord, I know there is more. I want to go beyond the veil, Lord. I want a more intimate relationship with You. Father, I want more! I want to know You more, I want to see You more, I want to experience You like never before."

I basically begged the Lord to show me more, give me more, satisfy the hunger I had for more of Him, and along the way to the more I was seeking, I became lost in darkness.

During that time, I was hearing more from the Lord, but my dreams became a battleground. Some dreams were so vivid that I began sleepwalking and talking in my sleep. Demons were sometimes chasing me, and I remember calling out the name of Jesus and crying out for help. My Aunt Lillie appeared in some of my dreams as an angel. I wasn't surprised by that at all because of the way God used her in my waking life to help me.

* * *

Scripture to use when seeking

Ask and it will be given to you; seek and you will find; knock and the door will be opened to you. For everyone who asks receives; the one who seeks finds; and to the one who knocks, the door will be opened. Matthew 7:7-8 (NIV)

Chapter 3

IT NEVER ENDS WELL WHEN MAN IS YOUR GOD

My life was plagued by the traumatic experiences of my childhood, and in my quest to find comfort, security, and love, I stumbled along the way. There were many boyfriends, and a few one-night stands I went through in search of the one who could rescue me from my brokenness. Maybe I was looking for the love I felt so long ago. I remember being asked by someone, "How is it that your mom was on drugs, and you didn't start using drugs?" The truth was, I didn't want to endure the torment that my mom endured, nor did I want my children to experience what I did. Let's be clear, I didn't make all the best decisions for my life, but I knew firsthand what drug addiction could do and I didn't want that for my children.

Even though drugs were not my portion, around every corner, I was looking for a man who would be my savior--I was lost in a sea of disappointment and encountered many men who I hoped would be the one. The broken me, the hungry me, and the me who felt abandoned in life, kept clinging to the hope that one day he would find me. My idea of love was the kind of love that my Aunt Lillie had always shown me—she always made sure I had something to eat. A person's worth to me was based on how they fed me. If they could feed me, in my eyes, they were golden. That simple act, one that most people take for granted, was the one thing that made me feel cared for.

That season of my life introduced a lot more guilt and shame--surrounding some of the decisions I made. When I was a freshman in college, I was a single mom with two little ones already, so when I got pregnant for the third time, I had an abortion because I felt I had no other choice. There was no way I could take care of another child. Later, I was with a guy who was in and out of jail, so I had no hope of building a future with him. I had two more abortions, and even though I only did what I thought was best, the guilt and shame lingered— packed away in a box, behind a door in my mind.

There came a time when I was no longer working at the strip clubs. I had a house of my own, and my mom was living with me. I made it clear I didn't want my daughters to grow up like I did, so as a condition of my mom living with me, she had to commit to never bringing drugs into my home. One day I came home and caught a whiff of that familiar smell, so

I put her OUT. At some point, she reached that final straw and quit for good. "What made you decide to quit?" I asked her. "I was tired." She had reached her "I AM DONE" moment and she never touched drugs again. Her strategy? She changed the places where she spent her time, the people she spent time with, and she changed the things she used to do. I told you my mom was amazing, smart, and determined!

My mom was finally drug free and was married to a man 10 years younger than her! He ADORED her! One year he threw her a birthday party and one of his co-workers, Marcus attended. When Marcus arrived, he walked in the front door, straight back to the kitchen where I was, and stood in the entryway. When I looked at him, I had a vision of me standing there in a wedding dress and took that as a sign that the muscular, good-smelling man whose clothes fit nicely on his body was my husband. I believed God was showing me that my search was over. Why else would I have that vision?

I had on a tight blue denim dress that stopped right above my knees. I was wearing a wet and wavy hairstyle, hazel contact lenses, and he liked what he saw. That night, we talked, and I drank for what seemed like hours. I had to stretch out on the couch because I drank too much, and he sat right there with me. We talked, and we talked. *Yeah. I think this is the one.*

After that night, we spent a lot of time together, and eventually made the relationship official. He was invited to stay with me at my house, but he never stayed more than a few nights at a time, which I couldn't understand. I felt rejected whenever he would leave because I couldn't figure out what was the problem. I considered myself to be an awesome woman who had her own place, I was pretty, and I was smart—so what was the problem?

One night when Marcus came over, he handed me his paycheck. *What on earth! This man is AMAZING! He worked all week and gave me all his money!* I felt like he was committed, by that gesture, to providing for me and my girls. Looking into in his eyes, I felt so much love between us, but the broken me, the hungry me, the me who felt alone and abandoned each time he decided to go home, couldn't shake that feeling of rejection when he left. I started to self-medicate with another person. I cheated.

We eventually separated for a few years before reconnecting at my stepdad's funeral. In the beginning, we spent a lot of time together, and when he wasn't at work, he was right by my side, helping me with the girls. He was the perfect support. One night, he popped the question. Looking into my eyes, with a warm smile he said, "I love you. Will you be my girlfriend?" *How could I say no?* Especially when I saw the desire in his eyes. By then, I had started my own business and was working it full-time. My income was intermittent, so Marcus took on the lion's share of the bills and household expenses. He made sure we had food to eat, and the rent was paid; however, there were subtle things happening that showed a crack in the relationship.

One night when he didn't come home, he told me he had a beer and was too drunk to drive home. The problem with that story was, I had never seen him take a drink. He began spending more time with his friends (going to amusement parks and parties) than he was spending with me, and when he was with me, we argued a lot. If I said up, he would say down. If I said wet, he would say dry. We lived in the same house together, but we were not living life together. To those on the outside looking in, we appeared to be a great couple, but I could feel the wall between us. I constantly told him how I loved him with my whole being. I was trying to break down the wall with my words. When we were intimate, I wanted him to know just how much he meant to me and said things like, "I put my life in your hands." I tried to cling to him with my words. I put him in a position of my god when I declared, "I no longer live for me, I live for YOU." Those words caused him to have such a hold on my life. Words are powerful, and I used my words to put that man above all.

The first time Marcus gave me a ring and asked me to marry him, I thought he was serious. One day while I was styling my daughter's hair, I took the engagement ring off. I was using a JAM hair product, and I didn't want it to get in the crevices of the ring. I sat the ring next to me, finished styling my daughter's hair, then went into the bathroom to wash my hands. When I returned, the ring was gone. There were about six kids running around at my mother's house at the time, and I didn't know if they played with it or if it had fallen in the chair. I just knew I couldn't find it and naturally, Marcus was upset.

I continued with planning the wedding, but Marcus was not involved in any of the planning or decision-making. He didn't even help set the date, so at some point I decided the wedding was off. I stayed with him, but the wedding was off.

The second time we began planning our wedding, he was more involved. We went together to check out the event venue and he paid the deposit. He listened as I added and subtracted names to and from the guest list, and I was excited that we were really going to do it this time. When we were less than three months away from the wedding, I asked about the fittings for his groomsmen and his tuxedo.

"I don't have time to worry about that s*%#!" he said. And with that, I canceled the wedding for a second time; but I still I didn't leave him.

Marcus knew how I felt about "shacking up." I wanted our relationship to be blessed by God, and he knew why I felt it was important that we be married. When he presented his mother's ring to me, with tears in his eyes, and asked me (for the third time) to marry him, I could not bring myself to say no, so I was willing to give our relationship one more try.

The third time around, we traded pictures back and forth about the themes and color schemes. We talked about different venues and what setting we wanted, and we even looked at fresh flower arrangements. He knew how much I loved fresh flowers. We did a lot of talking about the plans, but it seemed like all we did was talk. We never made any concrete plans. After a while, I sensed a disconnect, and it almost felt like I was being pacified—like he was just going through the motions, the whole time knowing it was just a façade.

I was working in my home office one day, thinking about the wedding plans, when the Lord gave me some specific instructions. I immediately walked upstairs to the bedroom where Marcus was lounging across the top of the bed watching TV. I sat at the bottom of the bed and said what the Lord had given me to say to him.

"It has been almost two years since you proposed. I told you I didn't want to live shacked up like this for the rest of my life, so if you really want to marry me, you will plan the wedding." I didn't know what to expect, but his response to that was, "What? I'm not planning a wedding, you do it."

I had already planned two weddings, so I told him I refused to let him make a fool out of me for the third time. I repeated the exact words the Lord had given me. "If you really want to marry me, like you said, you will plan the wedding."

For almost two years, we had the same conversation on multiple occasions, and each time, he gave a resounding "NO! Men don't plan weddings!" I had taken into consideration that he wouldn't know how to plan one, but I thought he would put forth some effort. He put a lot of effort into preparing to propose to me. He held secret conversations with my mom, daughters, sister, and even my cousin about the details of how, when, and where he would propose. I had expected that he might go back to them to ask questions about planning the wedding, so just in case, I asked them to let me know if he came to them to ask for help. At that point, I would have been willing and ready to take over the planning, but I really wanted to see him try. I wanted to see a sign that he really wanted to marry me. Instead, "No" was all I heard, time after time. My heart and my mind heard: *No, I don't love you enough to marry you. No, I don't love you enough to plan a wedding. No, I don't love you enough to come out of my comfort zone.*

I felt like I was being punished for the times early on in our relationship when I cheated on him. Something else had taken precedence over our relationship, and even though he tried to hide it, when I looked into his eyes, I saw nothing. That once loving smile had turned into a smirk.

He had always accused me of taking on the masculine role in the relationship. I never intended to overstep him, but because he was often silent and indecisive, I stepped up. One evening during Thanksgiving dinner, in my attempt to not take his role of man of the house away from him, I asked him to bless the food. He prayed.

"God is great, God is good, devil we thank you for this food." WAIT, WHAT?!

"I REBUKE THAT IN THE NAME OF JESUS!" my daughter and I yelled emphatically in unison. From that moment on, I couldn't look at him the same. What happened? I thought he was the one, but throughout our relationship, we both cheated, and it was not the vision God had given me. We separated for a while, but nothing I did or said fixed whatever it was that was broken in our relationship. So, after years of begging him to marry me, I was done. I was still hoping for more, but I was tired. I knew with him, this was as far as we could and would go.

❋ ❋ ❋

Scripture about other gods

You shall have no other gods before me. Exodus 20 ☺

Scripture to support self-worth

Do you not know that your bodies are temples of the Holy Spirit, who is in you, whom you have received from God? You are not your own; you were bought at a price. Therefore honor God with your bodies. I Corinthians 6:19-20

Scripture to combat worry

Do not be anxious about anything, but in every situation, by prayer and petition, with thanksgiving, present your requests to God. Philippians 4:6

Chapter 4

YOU'RE A WHAT?

I was ecstatic when I answered my front door and heard, "Hello, we'd like to talk to you about Jesus Christ." Finally! People with a passion for Jesus, and it wasn't even Sunday! I swung the door open and with a wave of my hand, I motioned for them to come in. I didn't realize how hungry I was for fellowship. More than anything, I was excited to have someone to talk to who shared my zeal for Jesus.

"Do you know the Lord Jesus?" the men asked me.

"Yes! I know that Jesus Christ died on the cross for the remission of my sins and rose again on the third day."

I was pleased at how I responded to their question with the script that had been programmed into my head. They shared with me the "Good News of Jesus Christ." I was so engrossed in the conversation; I don't remember if we talked for several minutes or several hours. They shared with so much passion and I was further intrigued when they highlighted certain Scriptures. For example, they explained the reference of "other sheep" (John 10:16) as those who were in the United States. Then, when they explained about the connection between the American Indians, the people of Africa, and the people in the United States, there was an explosion of excitement and curiosity inside of me, desiring to know more.

When it was time for them to leave, they asked if they could come back, and I said, "Of course! " I walked them to the door, grateful to have shared time and space with them, and as they left, one of them handed me the Book of Mormon.

"Ma, who were those guys and what were they doing here?" my daughter asked after they left.

"Girl, they are missionaries, and they want to talk about Jesus! They are supposed to come back, and I can't wait!"

They returned several times after that initial meeting, and my girls didn't like it one bit! I had to force my daughter Kelly to open the door to let them in.

"Kelly, why don't you like them?"

"I don't know, it's just something about them," she replied.

Whenever they came over, my other daughter, Sissy, would shake her head "no" and run into her room, but I made both of them sit down and listen. I did not want to repeat the same mistakes in my life, and I felt God had given me an opportunity--through those missionaries, to rebuild my relationship with Christ. I was adamant that my girls were going to go along with me on that journey. Kelly's body language and facial expressions told her true feelings. With her arms folded across her body, I could almost feel the wall of resistance as she positioned herself to not let their words penetrate in her mind. As they read from the Book of Mormon, I stuck with the only book I had ever known, my Bible.

The missionaries never had to worry about where their next meal was coming from or where they would sleep, because as they traveled all around sharing the "Good News," host families took care of them. That part of their experience tugged at my heart because they were being taken care of like I had always longed to be taken care of. They were a part of a family— the type of family I had been missing all my life. As we ate, worshipped, and studied together, it was a new take on what it meant to "belong." If I needed help around the house, the congregation was there to help. They lived a life dedicated to their beliefs, which was how I wanted my daily life to be. I wanted my life to reflect my love for Christ and my desire to follow Him. When they asked me about getting baptized, I jumped at what I saw as an opportunity to secure my salvation. The two missionaries who initially knocked on my door were the ones who dipped me in the water. After I got baptized, I took to the internet to learn more about my newfound family.

One of the first things my research turned up was stories about polygamy! That's right--one husband and many wives. *That will NOT be my life*, I quickly resolved in my mind. According to my Bible, Jesus never spoke about having multiple wives or growing a large family to secure one's place in Heaven, so I had questions. I began attending the group study sessions to get the answers and the way that it was explained to me, The *Fundamentalist* Church of Jesus Christ of Latter-Day Saints (FLDS) practiced polygamy, but we were The Church of Jesus Christ of Latter-day Saints (LDS) and did not practice polygamy. I put that in the back of my mind, but the more I studied the more questions I had.

The LDS belief was that when we go to Heaven, we become gods and goddesses. I didn't understand that part. There was something about becoming a goddess that sounded like a fairytale, and even though they believed in the holy trinity—God the Father, Jesus the Son, and the Holy Spirit, my spirit was troubled. Practicing that religion brought about more questions than answers, but I was intentional about doing the research, and I was not afraid to ask questions, even the difficult ones.

* * *

Scriptures about following other religions

Jesus answered, "I am the way, and the truth and the life. No one comes to the Father except through me. John 14:6 (ESV)

✳

For although there may be so-called gods in heaven or on earth—as indeed there are many "gods" and many "lords"—6 yet for us there is one God, the Father, from whom are all things and for whom we exist, and one Lord, Jesus Christ, through whom are all things and through whom we exist. 1 Corinthians 8:5-6 (ESV)

Chapter 5

READ - PONDER- PRAY

I was about thirty-six years old, and all my life I had believed God's teaching from the Bible. The one thing that kept coming to me was "thou shall have no other gods before me," and there I was practicing a religion that believed I was on track to becoming a god. That did not sit well with me. They also believed that after the resurrection and judgment, many would meet the requirements to achieve the highest level of salvation in the celestial kingdom, and from there, live eternally in God's presence. I wanted to gain a better understanding of how they would continue as familics in Heaven, become gods, create worlds, and have spirit children over which they would govern. I asked several times about it, but could not reconcile it in my mind or in my heart. Another blockbuster question came about when my research revealed that Mormons didn't like black people. What?! When those two missionaries knocked on my door, I am sure they noticed my skin color, but after reading article after article about how they did not allow blacks to become members, I wanted to bring my questions about that to the Bishop for clarity.

One of the things I liked about the church was that the Bishop made himself available to the congregation to talk and answer questions. After one of the church services, I let one of the church officials know I had a very important question for the Bishop. I was welcomed into his office, and as I began to ask my question, I was so nervous, but I managed to get it out.

"So I was online looking up information on Mormons," I began.

"This is all new to me, so I decided to do a little research."

The Bishop nodded and listened intently. I didn't know if he would think my question was silly, or if he would be embarrassed by it, but I was looking for understanding, so I continued.

"Well, I found an article on the internet that said the FLDS didn't like black people, and since they are the original church of LDS, I wanted to know what you thought."

According to the Bishop, the FLDS had a lot of beliefs that were not in alignment with what the LDS church believed. He assured me that their belief was that "Jesus loves all people and all are welcomed here." Before I left his office, he gave me a final piece of advice. "Read, ponder, and pray that you receive revelation from the Holy Spirit." That evening, that is exactly what I did. I opened the Book of Mormon and I read. I believed if I prayed, read, and pondered enough, God would give me the okay to accept the doctrine I was reading. That okay never came. After much prayer and pondering, all I could hear in my spirit was, "This is not for you." I didn't host the missionaries again after that. I stopped taking their calls and I never went back to that church.

The question I heard most was, "What? A Morman? How and why did you become a Mormon?" Then there were those who thought, "Oh you know Kim, she's crazy. She is always doing something flighty." The reality was, I loved Jesus Christ, and it was my desire to live my life every day filled with the knowledge of Him. The childhood encounter I had with the Holy Spirit was what I desired. I was in search of more of that.

* * *

Scripture on the importance of unity

. . . not giving up meeting together, as some are in the habit of doing, but encouraging one another—and all the more as you see the Day approaching. Hebrews 10:25 (NIV)

Scriptures on the importance of the true gospel

But even if we or an angel from heaven should preach a gospel different than the one we preached to you, let them be under God's curse! Galatians 1:8 (TPT)

*

Study to shew thyself approved unto God, a workman that needeth not to be ashamed, rightly dividing the word of truth. 2 Timothy 2:15 (KJV)

Chapter 6

WHAT ON EARTH
IS A CHRISTIAN WITCH?

I don't even remember how I got started in witchcraft, but I do remember that it was during the time when Marcus and I had been living together for a few years, and I was frustrated with my life. I was in a dark place, my relationship was broken, and I couldn't fix it. I had experienced a lifetime of trauma, and I was just looking for love, peace, and solutions.

I developed an interest in the movies about witches, werewolves, and vampires. I marveled at how witches could bend energy and change situations to their benefit, and I was fascinated about the immortality of werewolves and vampires. I felt drawn to those types of movies, but didn't understand how to respond. Those movie creatures seemed to have a control that I did not have, and I wanted it. I watched so many of those types of shows that my YouTube suggestions changed from what used to be a lot of technology-related content to content about manifesting and the supernatural.

When I was growing up, I always had a sense of "knowing." It was similar to characteristics portrayed by the witches I had seen in movies, not from a sermon on gifts of the Spirit or any teachings on a word of knowledge. They knew things about people without being told and they could say things and it would happen. That piqued my interest, and because I was always seeking knowledge, I sought out information about spiritual gifts, and how my gifts were related to my purpose. What is the point of these gifts? I didn't know if there was such a thing as a Christian witch, but I knew I was a Christian, I had dreams that came true, and I could speak things into existence.

In a nutshell, my research defined a Christian witch as one who believes in Jesus Christ, and uses tools of the occult to bring about change in their lives and in the lives of others. They use scriptures from the Bible, Christian icons, and images to produce spells and incantations. Tarot cards, crystals, and herbs are mixed into the practice to add potency to "the work." It is believed that an altar (a place used to conduct a ceremony, ritual, or sacrifice) should hold your Bible, tarot cards, and crystals.

I was ignorant when it came to that spiritual component. I thought that people considered Christians who exhibited spiritual gifts to be witches. I had no idea what I was getting myself into when my research led me to a particular self-proclaimed Christian witch who taught that it was okay to mix the Bible with crystals and tarot cards. I stayed up late watching her videos and consuming the content and felt like I had found the answer I had been looking for. When I found out about the mentorship program she offered to people who wanted to develop their spiritual gifts, I signed up IMMEDIATELY and wrote my first journal entry after joining that program:

> *"This is my first journal entry since joining this program and I guess I should start by explaining what this program is and how I became a part of it. If one subscribes to the law of attraction, one would assume that I attracted this group. Now that I am journaling, I believe I did. I started on a new path of spirituality, and I wanted a circle of sisters who were similar to me. I felt alone, like no one understood me and what I was experiencing. I wanted the comfort of a group of like-minded sisters. It's called a coven."*

Even though my religious experience taught me that being a witch or anything in that arena was sinful, my experience also taught me that there was more to God than what I was being taught in church. With my feet on a new path, I met several times a week with my coven of like-minded "sisters." A lot of what they shared with me was either very accurate or spot on concerning what I was dealing with in my life at that time. I was encouraged and embraced my new path as I tried to figure out what I was put on this earth to do.

It sounded harmless, but I was being taught that I was on equal footing with God and that I was a creator, just as God the Father. As a follower of Jesus Christ, I thought that was a very dangerous message. Encouraged by my coven sisters to begin writing a grimoire (a book of magic spells, incantations, and practices) I assembled reference material for the members of my family because I wanted to leave a legacy of learning so that they could understand their gifts. This was my first entry:

"I'm a child of God. I have been blessed with many gifts, my kids have gifts, my mom has gifts but there was no record of any other family members who were or are gifted and there are no records to teach me, so I am starting this for my family."

Listen, Satan is extremely strategic in his attacks. He's been on this earth longer than man and has watched us all that time. Please don't be fooled into thinking that Satan doesn't exist or that he can't develop a plan or scheme against you. He seeks to trap you and keep you trapped. On my path as a Christian witch, I heard so many spoken words that tickled my ear; words that piqued my interest and had me believing that I was on the path God wanted me on. I saw a video where a guy talked about how an angel had left a magic wand for him in the desert. The coach of our group talked about how her magic wand found her. I even thought my grimoire found me. The enemy made sure I experienced what I was being taught, as if to ensure that I thought this was from God. My language didn't change too much except I replaced "Holy Spirit" with the terms "spirit" or "universe." I changed my habit of reading my Bible to reading my daily horoscope instead. Not only did I read it, but I also subscribed to it, and I believed it word for word. I embraced and began living that lifestyle, and before I knew it, I had joined other groups I found on Meet-Up, whose focus was on witchcraft and all things in the occult. I took classes on how to create spells and dress candles. I paid to have my palm and cards read. I studied crystals and attended what they called a Drawing Down the Moon ceremony.

Honey!! The ceremony was held at night at the home of one of the members, and I didn't know anyone there. We all had an option of putting on a dark cloak (which was provided) or go naked. I chose to wear the cloak! I loved the theatrics of it. One by one, the participants put on the cloak, walked out into the backyard, joined the circle that had formed, and then started chanting. I thought it was strange and I felt out of place, but I continued.

As I looked around the circle of witches, most of them were intently focused, and others had speaking parts in the ritual. One of the older, more experienced women in the practice (Crone) stepped into the middle of the circle to "speak for the moon" from the energy we had supposedly drawn down. I remember praying for some type of revelation; that the Crone would say something specifically to me; perhaps a word of guidance. Surely God would show Himself to me again. My childhood encounter with the Holy Spirit left me feeling seen, acknowledged, and known. While I was standing in the circle, hoping for a word from the moon, the Crone looked right past me. I didn't feel seen or heard, and I left feeling just as empty as I did when I arrived.

On another occasion, I participated in an astral projection ceremony. Astral projection refers to an out-of-body experience during which the spirit leaves the body and travels in the spirit realm. It is ILLEGAL. While one person was beating on drums, another person did a guided meditation that led us out of our natural bodies, and allowed our spirits to roam. I was excited. I remember rising out of my body and looking at everyone seated on the floor around me. I then walked down through the floor, down a set of stairs and approached a red door. I walked through the door and looked around at the new space I just entered, and it was like a forest with tall trees and green grass. There was a dirt path I felt compelled to take and I saw an arch made with two thick pillars holding a signpost across the top. Engraved on the signpost were ancient symbols called runes (used for magic, divination, and writing). There was a girl there who motioned me to come in further, and I walked through the archway. I NEVER should have done that!

I began to have more and more visions. In one of the visions, I was in an Indian village that had large teepees. A young girl lifted the edge of one of the teepees and showed me the inside of it. I saw a mortar and pestle set and thought that meant that perhaps I was a medicine woman in a past life. I believed what I saw in the visions, and before long, I had set up altars in my house one for doing work and the other to honor my ancestors. I had shelves of herbs, crystals, and candles for casting spells. I purchased books to help me as I did work for people, and had soon attracted the attention of a demon who visited me in a dream.

* * *

I was watching some kind of ritual or ceremony being conducted by a shaman, regarded as having access to and influence in the world of good and evil spirits. From one side of the room, I was watching and from another side of the room I was working with a family. The family (father, mother, and a daughter) were doing a reading on me. At the same time, the shaman was performing some type of ceremony while communicating with the spirits. During the ceremony, a very powerful dark spirit took an interest in me—it was watching me as I watched the dream. It moved closer to where I was and when it did, I was frozen with fear. I wanted to be invisible. How could he even see me? Why was he attracted to me?

I held my breath hoping I would wake up from the nightmare. The thought never crossed my mind to call out Jesus' name. I somehow managed to turn and walk away, but the demon followed me. I could feel his hunger for me. It almost felt like he savored seeing me and looked forward to consuming my soul. The family doing my reading was afraid to tell me what was revealed, but the shaman told me it meant I would die within two to three years. I was devastated.

The fear I felt in that dream stuck with me in my awakened state, and I couldn't shake it. I felt a heaviness in my home, and chaos and turmoil in my mind. Later, I had another dream.

✱   ✱   ✱

I had gone to the store and was standing in line waiting to check out. A very tall man walked in and stood directly behind me. At first, I didn't recognize him, but I turned to say hello. He didn't respond. I realized I didn't know him, so I spoke again. In a very stern voice he said, "I know you." I smiled as I said, "I'm only saying hi," and then he said, "Hello." It was understood that we weren't going to discuss how he knew me, but I thought he might be my cousin on my dad's side who had passed away.

That dream was confirmation that demons were watching me, and it only added to the darkness that was growing inside me. Those dreams were an indication I had opened the door to that type of activity, and that was the reason I felt so separated, lost, and so disconnected from life, from God. I initially thought the confusion resulted from my life, in general, but it was really a reflection of how far away I had moved from God. It felt like death. I had touched the unclean things. My dreams revealed that my actions and words had given familiar spirits (which had been passed down through the bloodline) permission to take up residence. I had no understanding of generational curses, how to identify them, or how to break them, so I lived with the torment. In a matter of months, I found myself facing nights where I really didn't want to go to sleep. I started to feel that familiar sense of loss--like I had no sense of direction and had forgotten my purpose.

I was on a roller coaster ride of emotions. Just a few months prior, I was on cloud nine after completing a 21-day fasting and journaling assignment. The assignment brought me a sense of clarity and purpose, but I was back at that dark place again. I was desperately seeking wisdom and guidance from, "The Divine," so I walked around with a journal ready to capture the revelation when it came.

Journaling was an excellent tool that helped me to unburden my brain by writing down my thoughts. Not only did I have my own thoughts to deal with, but I thought I could hear other people's thoughts as well. I was suffering in my thought life, and I didn't realize how living my life so separated from God had taken a toll on my physical body. I went from always having stamina, drive, and motivation to having to force myself to move; sometimes barely being able to eat and take a bath. I felt empty inside.

During that time, I had taken a year off from my business to care for my new grandson. Although I had moved far away from God, He still reached out for me. I had another dream.

* * *

I was driving along a road that I had driven many times before, and while driving, I fell asleep at the wheel. (I was having a dream inside of a dream). My grandson was awake in the back seat, a cop was behind me, a huge truck was on my right, and the median strip was on my left. I didn't crash or have an accident, and the cop didn't pull me over. I woke up in the dream and continued driving.

When I woke up from the dream, I reflected on it in real time and thought: *Is God trying to warn me about the path I'm on? Is he trying to show me that the path is dangerous, not just for me, but for my grandchildren? Were my actions opening or holding open doors for generational curses?*

Later that year, just like clockwork, I found myself off track again. I was broke. My company wasn't bringing in any money, and I had a ton of bills due. I was ready to give up the mess of a life that I had made for myself. One night, I was watching TV, lethargically laying on the couch, I prayed, *Lord, why is this always happening to me and how can I get back on track?* A simple prayer. I peeled myself away from the couch, gathered my purse, my journal, and my laptop, and headed for bed. I usually played nature sounds to help me relax, but I decided to listen to something inspirational instead. I wanted to be inspired by successful people, and asked myself: *Who should I listen to first?* I was focused on self, when "self" could not even get me out of bed in the morning. At no point did I open my Bible or wait to hear the Lord's answer to my prayer. My soul wasn't connected. Steve Jobs popped into my head.

I didn't realize how being involved in witchcraft had severely screwed my life up. I went through so many cycles of depression, and feeling lost and alone. Instead of seeking God, I forgot all about Him, and even when I did pray, I didn't listen for His answer. When I heard that there was going to be a convention in Baltimore for black witches, I was excited to attend. Surely this was my tribe. I should be able to get answers here: *Spirit would show up for me here, right?* On the day of the convention, I stood in line--full of anticipation, smiling at the other ladies who all seemed to be as eager as I was. The convention was the first of its kind in our area and it was packed to capacity with women from all over. A variety of classes were offered, including classes on candle magic, crystals, traditional African religions and the Orishas. Orishas are spirits that play a key role in the Yoruba religion of West Africa and several of the African diaspora that derive from it. The attendees had an opportunity to speak with a high priestess who was doing readings. I stood in that long line to receive a reading, and based on the reactions of the women ahead of me, whatever the woman said to them must have been extremely accurate.

When I was the third person in line, my excitement grew. Two more people, then it would be my turn. There were tears and *"Thank you so much."* One more person to go, *Hugs and laughter*, then I stepped up to the table to listen to what the high priestess had to say to me.

"Your ancestors are upset with you. They aren't speaking to you. You need to spend more time on your altar. Pray to them more, feed them every day, put stuff on your altar that they like. Give it some time. That should work."

I received what the high priestess said to me. I believed my ancestors weren't speaking to me because they frowned on what I was doing. I was conflicted about the altars I set up in my house. The scriptures speak about "honoring thy mother and father." So wasn't I honoring them by setting up an altar to honor my loved ones who had gone on to be with the Lord? I was confused.

I used to receive prayer requests from people who knew me. They requested prayer for jobs, healing, and peace in their homes because they knew I could get a prayer through. I paid for the material I used for their prayers (herbs and candles) out of my own pocket, and I didn't charge them for the prayer materials. I know that part about the candle magic might ruffle a few feathers, but people use candle magic all the time. At birthday celebrations, when you make a wish and blow out the candles (make sure you blow them all out in one breath)—that's candle magic. I'm just saying. If I told you the origins of half the stuff we do that is rooted in pagan religions, or the worship of other gods, especially as Christians, it would blow your mind! Most believers practice witchcraft and don't realize it. Witchcraft: the malevolent act of invoking or speaking of incantations to control people or events by supernatural means.

* * *

Scriptures about witchcraft

Regard not them that have familiar spirits, neither seek after wizards, to be defiled by them: I am the LORD your God. Leviticus 19:31 (KJV)

*

But the fearful, and unbelieving, and the abominable, and murderers, and whoremongers, and sorcerers, and idolaters, and all liars, shall have their part in the lake which burneth with fire and brimstone: which is the second death. Revelation 21:8 (KJV)

*

For rebellion is as the sin of witchcraft, and stubbornness is as iniquity and idolatry. Because thou hast rejected the word of the LORD, he hath also rejected thee from being king. I Samuel 15:23 (KJV)

*

Now the works of the flesh are manifest, which are these; Adultery, fornication, uncleanness, lasciviousness, 20 Idolatry, witchcraft, hatred, variance, emulations, wrath, strife, seditions, heresies, 21 envyings, murders, drunkenness, revellings, and such like: of the which I tell you before, as I have also told you in time past, that they which do such things shall not inherit the kingdom of God. Galatians 5:19-21(KJV)

Chapter 7

TORMENTED

In the spring of 2017, I found myself in a familiar place. I was having plenty of thoughts, feelings, and emotions; yet, I felt like I had nothing to write about. When I did try to write in my journal, as soon as I gripped the pen, I felt a surge of tension, and a pull of the muscles down from my forearm. I could not understand why there was so much physical tension associated with my writing hand.

In writing, there is reflection; in reflection there is acknowledgement; and in acknowledgement there can be deliverance. I felt trapped and could feel my soul crying out for freedom. I wanted to see the real me, but I was weighed down with so many dark, heavy, suffocating layers of what was not me. The Holy Spirit was nudging me to write.

Why do I hurt so bad and feel so unworthy? If I knew, really knew, I could do something about it; I could make a change for the better.

When I looked at my accomplishments on paper, they were amazing! I was phenomenal! But in spite of what it looked like on paper, it was almost like I was looking at another person who was separate from me. The feeling that I was totally lost was weighing me down. I didn't know who I was anymore, and I was really struggling with why I needed to feel accepted.

* * *

Scriptures of torment and worry

See, LORD, how distressed I am! I am in torment within, and in my heart I am disturbed, for I have been most rebellious. Outside, the sword bereaves; inside, there is only death. Lamentations 1:20 (NIV)

*

Cast all your anxiety on him because he cares for you. I Peter 5:7 (NIV)

For as long as I can remember, my family would pack up the car and take a ride to attend our family reunions. Twenty-five years ago, it took us seven hours to drive from Baltimore, Maryland to South Boston, Virginia. I absolutely loved the long drive. Peering out the window, I would watch as the trees and wide-open grassy fields flew by. Our family used to always reunite on my uncle's property during the summer. As we pulled into the driveway, I could see his house sitting a few yards off the main road with large trees peppered around the front of the property. My uncle's son's house sat to the right of his, and his daughter's house sat to the left. He owned acres and acres of farmland that stretched far beyond the houses. Wandering around the sides of the main house led to a breathtaking view. Open fields extended all the way back to a forest, which was also a part of his property. There were pig pens, a large barn, structures for slaughtering farm animals, and for processing the tobacco that was grown on the farm, and an outhouse! The front yard was massive. There was a covered structure that the men constructed to offer protection from the sun and rain. We would set up the food there, and most of the elders congregated under it to talk and laugh while the children explored the country and all it had to offer.

There were so many of us that it was hard to find a spot to sit or stand inside. Some gathered in the living room of the main house, but no matter where we were, laughter and stories of the past could be heard reverberating through the house and around the property. There was always a baby sleeping on the bed with scores of cousins "listening out for the baby."

As soon as we arrived, unpacked the car, and said hello to everyone, I would kick my shoes off and relax! I was filled with so much joy that it felt like my heart could burst! I have always felt a connection to the land. I loved the wide-open spaces, experiencing the cool breeze blowing across my skin, the feeling of grass under my feet, and the sway of the trees in the wind. It blesses me just to know that everything around me is alive as nature reveals that we are not alone. Observing God's influence and the beauty of His creation always makes me feel close to God, so being surrounded by nature's mere presence warms my heart and puts a smile on my face.

Each year, I regretted we only stayed for a weekend, because I wanted to stay much longer. Two days in paradise were never enough for me. In the back of my mind, I planned to buy my slice of Heaven and live every day just like I did during the two short days with family.

As the years rolled by, we grew older, had families of our own, and we started to stay in hotels instead of at my uncle's house. Still, I loved sitting in his front yard. It didn't matter how late it got or how sleepy I was. I would have slept in the yard if I could. The smell of the wood burning as they roasted the pig that would be served for dinner filled the air. I found the entire family reunion experience to be calming and comforting.

Life pushed in and I stopped going to the family reunion for a while, but in the summer of 2019, I went back, and I was so happy to be there! About three days after I returned from an amazing experience with my family at a place that brought me so much joy, peace, and happiness, I felt full of nothingness. That's weird, right?

Three days earlier, I was full of joy and felt refreshed, but that had changed once I got settled in back at home. In just three days, I had no drive, no joy, no get up and go. The only thing I felt was emptiness. I was baffled. I mean, I was forty-seven years old, and I had no idea where my happiness was or what even made me happy. Questions swirled in my mind constantly. *What is wrong? Why am I unhappy? Why do I keep finding myself in this place? Does God hear me? Why is it that nothing I do leads me to a better state of being?* I moved along robotically, and the word "pivot" kept appearing. Whether I was reading an article or scrolling on social media, I kept seeing the word "pivot." When I was in meetings, I was hearing "pivot." *Was God speaking to me?* So I Googled it.

My life needed a pivot. I needed to make a change in the way I was living. The best way for me to pivot (I thought) was to break my life into sections and to start one step at a time. I began to take a deeper look into each facet of my life to determine what I needed to do to get out of the depression I found myself in. I wanted to execute at my fullest potential in every area of my life, so I grabbed my journal and listed out each area of my life I needed to examine and get back on track.

On page one, I wrote: "Spirituality." What does my spiritual practice look like?" On the next page I wrote: "Business. What does my business look like?" I repeated that for the other areas, like my home life, family, wealth, legacy, and health. In considering the changes I needed to make, I didn't factor in, "seek ye first the kingdom of God and his righteousness and all these things shall be added unto you."

During that time, I was calling myself a creator, boasting I had the ability to create. I dug deep into that false belief. Please understand, we do create situations for ourselves which are the result of our decisions—the decisions we make and the decisions that we don't make. It is not the same as operating under that belief. That is something completely different. There are those who honestly believe they are equal to the Creator God Elohim. They are operating under a false belief, that I am God, and I make my reality by thinking they are equal to the Creator and have the ability to create their own reality. I mean, isn't that why Lucifer was kicked out of Heaven?

Let's park right here for a second.

Then God said, 'Let us make mankind in our image, in our likeness, so that they may rule over the fish in the sea and the birds in the sky, over the livestock and all the wild animals, and over all the creatures that move along the ground.' Genesis 1:26 (NIV)

We were given dominion of the earth; however, in order to exercise that dominion in the manner God intended, we must walk in the authority given to us by the Holy Spirit after we accept Jesus as our Savior.

✳ ✳ ✳

Scripture on repentance

If my people, which are called by my name, shall humble themselves, and pray, and seek my face, and turn from their wicked ways; then will I hear from heaven, and will forgive their sin, and will heal their land. 2 Chronicles 7:14 (KJV)

Chapter 8

FOR I KNOW THE PLANS
I HAVE FOR YOU

I was raised in church, and I loved everything about it. I loved the joy of coming together with everyone, and I loved the music. When I was not at church, I played church with my younger cousins, Katina, who was the usher, and Sherry, who sang! We had our own little church, and I preached from a book we all had entitled "My Book of Bible Stories." On Saturday, my Aunt Lillie sent a message to my other aunts to have us kids ready on Sunday morning. "I'm going to come through and blow the horn," she would say. I loved going to church to hear more about this miraculous person that loved us and could do anything if we just believed in Him. I spent the weekends at my Aunt Lillie's house, so when she made her rounds to pick up the others, I was already in the car.

At the end of the service, we all went to the dining room, located in the basement, and ate. The dining room was always filled with other church members, children running around, older kids hanging out in the lounge of the women's bathroom, and everyone laughing and communing with one another.

My aunt was an usher, and I admired how structured she and the other ushers were. Their white uniforms made me think of what heavenly garments would look like; and when they marched in, they marched on one accord with precision and grace. There were about five cousins and myself who sang in the choir, and after the birth of my second child, I became an usher.

On the first Sunday that I was scheduled to usher, I had to borrow a uniform (that didn't fit) and shoes (that were too big). No one mentioned the fact that my shoes were so big that they flipped off my feet, or that my usher uniform didn't fit, but there was something about not being prepared and being unpolished that made me feel ashamed. That was my first and last ushering experience.

I continued to show up with my two girls for Sunday service, and I attended the women's ministry classes. Determined to take a stand for Jesus and live holy, I threw out my secular music, movies, and books, and I even changed the way I dressed. I knew there was something specific I was designed to do, but I had no idea what it was. I continued to press in, asking God to reveal His plan for my life. A mistake we often make in prayer is asking God a question, jumping up and leaving without waiting for God's response. I continued to ask God for a revelation, and in true fashion, He answered me in a dream.

* * *

I was walking across a field of beautiful green grass. The sky was blue, and the sun was bright. I was happy, full of joy, and I felt loved. As I continued walking across the field, I noticed a large structure in the distance, laying in the grass. When I got closer to it, I could see a man nailed to the structure. Suddenly, the structure (a cross) lifted off the grass, and as it moved into an upright position I heard, "Lift him up . . . Lift him up". I stood at the base of that huge wooden cross and when I looked up at it, it stretched up as far as I could see up into the sky. The crossbeam stretched wide and looked like outstretched arms waiting to embrace a welcome friend. I stood in amazement gazing at the cross.

I didn't know how or when I was going to do it, but I knew for sure that my assignment was to "lift him up." In order for me to carry out that assignment, I needed to strengthen myself against the pull of the flesh, and I needed the Holy Spirit to guide me completely. I made my declaration that my life would serve as a testimony that when you accept Christ, you are transformed into a new creature, and I was being transformed.

*   *   *

Scripture of encouragement

16 The face of the Lord is against those who do evil, To cut off the memory of them from the earth. 17 When *the righteous* cry [for help], the Lord hears And rescues them from all their distress *and* troubles. 18 The Lord is near to the heartbroken And He saves those who are crushed in spirit (contrite in heart, truly sorry for their sin). Psalm 34:16-18 (AMP)

Chapter 9

SURRENDER

A sense of dread came over me as soon as I made that right turn into my neighborhood. I felt so blessed to have found our single-family detached home that sat on a little less than half an acre of land. For city living, that was amazing! The home was big enough to host my family inside and out for birthday or holiday parties. Four bedrooms with two bathrooms was more than enough room for me and Marcus, my two girls, and my two grandkids. There was even a formal dining room I turned into a playroom for the grands, before turning it into my home office.

My home was once a place of peace, but I could feel the weight of oppression on me as soon as I opened the front door. I would go to work and come home; and there were a few times when I came home from work and sat in the truck to gather my thoughts. I would take a deep breath, turn off the truck, and walk down the walkway to the front porch. It was not uncommon for me to sit out there for hours with a good book and a glass of wine, lighting up my chiminea on the colder nights.

One day, it all came down on me. I had become bitter and angry and could no longer tolerate living in the turmoil of our relationship. I kept hoping God would show up and answer my prayer. *You answered my prayers and delivered my mom from her addiction, but now, I need you to rescue me. Do you see what I'm going through?* I was tired, frustrated, and had lost hope at the end of my rope. As soon as I stepped through the door, I could feel the weight of the oppression come on me. It pushed my shoulders forward, and I slumped as I walked up the steps to my bedroom.

I laid on the bed next to Marcus with my heart filled with disappointment at what felt like wasted years of our relationship. For years, I had made that man my God. I did what I could to be the woman he wanted and the woman he could be proud of. I had made him my God and given my life over to him.

As I laid next to him with my eyes closed, silently crying, I balled myself up into a fetal position, pulling my knees close to my chest and tucked my head. The tears soaked my pillow as I thought -- *Does he know I'm dying inside? Can he see the darkness that is consuming me? Does he even care I have lost my will to live?*

The many years of giving my very life over to Marcus left me empty. Not knowing what he wanted, or what would make him love me enough to marry me left me with feelings of unworthiness. I was tired of carrying the shame, and I was so ashamed of what my life had become.

I felt myself wallowing in self-pity and it became harder for me to breathe as I continued to lay there, trying not to let him hear me cry. That was insane. He was the one who did it to me; *Why did I feel a need to protect him from the pain of my emotions?*

How did I even get here? Why did this happen to me? How had I gotten so far off course?

I thought I was a good person. I didn't cause trouble or stir up chaos. I was someone who people could depend on, and I was generous with my money. What awful thing did I do to deserve this?

I laid there, at the brink of death and I quietly pleaded with God to honor one final request. *Please don't let my daughters find me here dead.*

The Holy Spirit must have interceded on my behalf. I felt the Lord say, "Enough is enough, Daughter. This is not the life I have planned for you. You will not die here."

It didn't matter, I had already made my peace with God.

It took that moment of complete surrender for the process of reconciliation to take place. I began to understand that some experiences come to strip away, or rip away false doctrine and beliefs and they lay to rest behaviors and habits that no longer serve you. Some experiences come to develop and fortify you. It's those experiences we find most painful. We must realize that holding on to familiar pain, maintaining broken relationships or beliefs we no longer subscribe to, ultimately turn us into someone other than who we know we should be. Rather than letting go of painful things, we sometimes cling to them because they bring some form of comfort.

During the spring of 2020, I was invited by my cousin to attend a retreat. She had attended the year before and spoke very highly of the retreat's founder and about the spiritual elevation she received as a result of attending. I jumped at the opportunity. I'm not sure if my cousin knew I had been burning candles and messing with herbs and crystals, or maybe the Holy Spirit told her to share it with me. Whatever the reason, I recognized the opportunity as one I needed to grab with both hands.

I signed up for VIP status at the retreat as I felt a hunger for the Lord begin to rise within me. I remembered a plea I made to the Lord for a closer relationship, a more authentic experience, and a stronger anointing. Everyday leading up to the time of the retreat, I spoke to myself several times a day in anticipation of what was to come. I knew I was going to be able to not just hear from the Lord, but be touched by Him. The anticipation was growing, and I was expecting a mighty move to occur at the retreat.

My cousin and I fasted two days before the retreat to prepare ourselves mentally, spiritually, and physically to receive what we needed. I was serious about having another chance to hear from the Lord. I wanted to be cleansed and purified, and I saw the retreat as my chance to feel His love once again, and know that He sees me. It was my chance to feel relevant.

The theme of the retreat was "Purification." However, I needed to get in alignment to be purified. When you are aligned, things flow better. When you are aligned with the right people surrounding you, there is more liberty for you to share the things that are going on in your life. I know it is not wise to tell your business to just anybody and everybody, but through the discernment of the Holy Spirit, you can get in alignment with people whose conversations will not only edify you, but will help bring you in closer alignment with your goals. All of this will ultimately lead to your success.

* * *

Scriptures of Surrender

28 "Come to me, all you who are weary and burdened, and I will give you rest. 29 Take my yoke upon you and learn from me, for I am gentle and humble in heart, and you will find rest for your souls. 30 For my yoke is easy and my burden is light." Matthew 11:28-30 (NIV)

Chapter 10

HE SAW ME

T he retreat was held on a mountain, and that is where I felt seen—on the mountaintop!

We were already prepared in our minds and in our spirits to receive whatever it was the Holy Spirit wanted to impart to us during the retreat. When we arrived, we received our VIP swag bag that contained a journal that had been prayed over prior to the event by the hosting committee. Each attendee received a journal that was specifically designed and contained a message written just for them. My journal was pink, and written in gold were the words taken from Psalm 46:1, "God is within her, she will not fail," and my special message read:

> "Kimberly, the Lord is inviting you to receive the very best of Him; not just what He can bless you with, but He wants to fill the deepest depths of your soul. He wants to consume you. Yield to Him, give Him access to every part of you, and you will see your life

transformed. He has so much in store for you. He is the answer and solution to all you have in mind. Be steadfast, both in private and in public. Stay encouraged. Obey. He has you, in Jesus' name."

❀   ❀   ❀

Scripture on God's plans for you

For I know the plans and thoughts that I have for you,' says the Lord, 'plans for peace and well-being and not for disaster, to give you a future and a hope. Jeremiah 29:11 (AMP)

Chapter 11

CUT AWAY ANYTHING THAT IS NOT LIKE YOU

S o often I've prayed "*Lord, cut away anything that is not like you*," but I don't think I ever expected things to go. When I turned back to Christ, it was my sincere desire to really live as a woman of God. I wanted to do what the Lord had called me to do. In my prayers, I literally felt like I broke my heart open and poured its contents out at His feet. I asked Him to satisfy my desire to live righteously, and I asked Him to make me clean. I had an unyielding pull to live a life worthy of the sacrifice of Christ, and one of the major changes I knew I needed to make was to sever the relationship I had with Marcus.

Our relationship of almost twenty years, consisted of three marriage proposals, off and on engagements, canceled wedding plans, but never a wedding. All of that had me at my lowest point, and just a few months before attending the retreat I laid in bed feeling my life was over.

We arrived on the very first day of the retreat, full of expectation and excitement. My cousin and I were both brimming with anticipation of what was in store for us. As the attendees got comfortable with our weekend environment, we were each given an opportunity to share who we were and what we expected to receive from the retreat. That set an atmosphere of expectation among us. We were all gathered at that sacred and anointed place expecting to be blessed by God, and being there physically was a blessing for me because I knew the presence of God was there. On that first day, I discovered something about myself. I was hiding a lot.

I was hiding behind shame. I was carrying a lot of shame that could very well have been planted by unclean spirits that tormented me for years while I was practicing witchcraft.

I was also hiding behind my family. I was hiding behind what I thought my role was in the family which resulted in me denying myself by always saying yes to whatever my family asked of me.

On day two of the retreat, my cousin and I were seated at a table eating our lunch when one of the other retreat attendees joined us. I didn't know her or anything about her, but as we were finishing our meals, she asked me a question.

"Are you married?"

"No," I answered.

"Are you involved?" she continued.

"It's complicated," I said, abruptly getting up from the table and finding a seat on a nearby couch to write in my new journal. After a few minutes my cousin came over to me and tried to convince me to come back to the table. "She has something she wants to tell you," she said of the woman who had so many questions. I reluctantly went back to the table and after I took a seat, the woman asked my cousin to hold an empty chip bag and an empty soda can in one hand. She then directed her to pick up the empty plate and napkin with her other hand. With both of my cousin's hands full of trash, the woman attempted to hand her a cell phone and I could see her struggling to figure out a way to grab it. That's when the woman directed her conversation to me.

"I knew you weren't married. I just started the conversation with you that way because I wanted to let you know what the Lord is saying to you." She had my attention! Then she proceeded to give me the message.

"God says 'He is trying to give you something better, but it's like you're holding on to emptiness; to things that need to be thrown away or gotten rid of. The things that your hands are clenching to, you need to release so that you can receive the things He has for you. He says, 'Your time in that relationship

is over. There is someone else who is waiting for you, but you must release what you are holding onto."

What the woman said to me was confirmation. For years I heard the words, "You are holding on to the very thing I am trying to rip from your hands." The first time I heard it, was one day when I was driving home. I'm not sure why my attention was drawn to it, but I noticed I had a death grip on the steering wheel. As soon as I noticed how tightly I was gripping the wheel, I heard those same words: "You are holding on to the very thing I am trying to rip from your hands." After that, I would see images of my fist clinched tightly and I would hear those exact words again. The woman's message confirmed that I was indeed hearing from the Lord.

As soon as the woman left our table, my cousin and I had a conversation about everything the woman had said.

"Guurrlll, I knew it!" my cousin said. "When she asked you if you were married, I *knew* she was going to have a word for you!"

For the next few minutes, we marveled at the way the woman delivered the message using the same imagery that the Lord had already shown me. I had been in a car accident earlier in the year, and I was sure that my back had been severely damaged. I had several MRIs scheduled, and even went as far as laying on the table about to be pushed into the machine when I said, "Nope, I can't do it."

When the woman mentioned I was having issues with my back, I knew there was no way she could have known that, except that God revealed it to her.

"You can be healed whenever you want to. Just lay out on the floor," she told me. I agreed with her and decided I would be healed, but not right then, because I was not stretching out on that floor in front of all those strangers.

We were given an assignment on the second day of the retreat. On day two of the retreat, our assignment was to consume the Word of God. I knew I needed to surrender my fears to Him. I wanted to be intentional about finding my community, and it was not a coven of witches, or a family unit of Mormons. I belonged to a community of believers who loved and followed Jesus Christ.

In a one-on-one conversation I had with our hostess, the Holy Spirit gave her words I needed to hear as I was finding my way back to Christ. God was stripping away layer upon layer as He revealed things I had not seen before, like how I had assumed the position of God in the lives of those closest to me, when that was not my role. He also allowed me to see how I had placed others in the position of God in my life, and that was not their role. I had gotten so caught up in the blessing that God had given me at a particular time in my life that I started to idolize the person. In doing so, I lost sight of God.

By day three (the last day of the retreat) I had fully repented for how I had hardened my heart against God, and it was the beginning of a brand new day. I had poured out all my hurt and pain; all my loneliness and anything else that was weighing me down. I knew things had shifted within me. I had a real desire to be in alignment with the Word of God, and I knew that living in a situation where I would be tempted with sexual immorality was defiant and rebellious. Sex out of wedlock had to end, and I was okay with that.

God describes death as being separated from Him, and in my relationship with Marcus, I was separated from God. That's why I felt like I was dying. It was in that relationship I was most separate from God. My home had become a nest of chaos and turmoil, and I believe it was all due to my relationship with the darkness. It had taken up residence. Once I was able to let go of that relationship and Marcus moved out of the house, the whole energy and atmosphere in the house changed. I went through the house praying and anointing the windows and doors. I got rid of all the occult items I had gathered over the years. All the candles, crystals, herbs, and everything associated with the occult, or my former witchcraft practice had to go! There are serious consequences for dabbling in illegal spiritual practices like witchcraft, and such actions lead to spiritual and physical death. It is a road that leads to mental torment and anguish of the body, and although there are those who may not believe in demons and imps, they do exist, and they believe what God has said about us. In fact, their very existence is to derail us and send us to hell. I charged the angels to encamp around my home and stand guard at every entryway. I knew I was protected. I felt protected.

My experience in finding my way back to Jesus Christ taught me quite a few things. Mainly, there is no substitute for the Holy Spirit. My life immediately changed after my mountaintop experience at that retreat. I began experiencing the spirit of peace, joy, and love as the Holy Spirit ministered to me. He ministered to me in my sleep, and I started my days just sitting quietly, seeking His guidance. My mind always had so many thoughts running through it, but I set aside that quiet time just to sit with the Lord. I changed the words I was speaking and began to speak life, healing and Christ over me and my life. I was diligently consuming the Word of God and seeking Him from a fresh perspective. I always reflect to those early years when my Aunt Lillie introduced me to the Lord by taking me to church, talking to me about Jesus, listening to my dreams, and teaching me that my connection to Jesus was through prayer. As early as eight years old, I was developing my own intimate relationship with the Lord. I knew Jesus Christ was my Lord and Savior, and I knew that the Bible was God's Word. After returning from the retreat,

I positioned myself to have an even deeper, more intimate relationship with God and began by consuming His Word.

In my pursuit of more of God, I came across a video of Cora Jakes Coleman talking about the many names of God. I already knew Him to be Jehovah Jireh (one of His many names), based on the many times when there was no money for food, but he provided food. There were times when we were homeless, but I saw God's provision as He touched the heart of a landlord who gave us favor. I thought about the many moments along my journey where the Lord showed up, and as gratitude filled my heart, my relationship with Him grew even stronger. I started having praise and worship sessions in my car on my commutes, and I spent time talking and communing with the Holy Spirit as I drove.

There were times when I felt a sense of condemnation when I thought about how I participated in idol worship by putting people in the place of God in my life. I thought about my past practices in witchcraft and all the things I had done in the past, and sometimes those thoughts tried to put a wedge between me and the Lord, but I was in a new place in Christ, and I could clearly hear the Holy Spirit saying, "Don't keep begging and dwelling on the past, you have been forgiven."

A few months later, my cousin and I attended another women's conference. I felt really drawn to one of the speakers, so I attended the breakout session she hosted. In that session, there were things spoken by her I had been thinking and feeling that only God knew. I knew that her message to me was from God. In part, she said:

There is a calling on your life, and you've been running from it for a long time. There is shame you must release before you can flow in your gift. God has already forgiven you and it is forgotten. God has heard your petition, and it is done. You have to believe that you are forgiven and that has been something you have struggled with. You are about to dig deep in His Word, and He will provide clarity. You won't be in that confused, "I don't understand, I don't know what's going on mindset. Satan is attacking your mind. He is attacking and coming against you because of your gift and your anointing. You have dreams--you have a Prophet Jeremiah anointing. Your heart is right, but Satan is attacking your mind and is coming against you because of your anointing. God has to get it all lined up.

When the Woman of God was finished speaking over me, all I could do was bless God for His Word and for his Holy Spirit. I received God's Word as it was spoken by his servant and I wrote in my journal, "Yes God. My soul says yes. Generational curses stop with me."

The Lord was not done. He had a Word for me in the second session as well. He confirmed His Word through another prophetess who spoke encouragement into my life. In part, she said:

> *The shame has kept you in the back, but God is calling you to the front. You like to stay in the back, and it's because of the shame, but God says, "No more! Stop running! When you leave this conference, things will be different. I can hear you say, 'Yes, Lord,' in the spirit."*

* * *

Scriptures on faith and forgiveness

If we confess our sins, he is faithful and just and will forgive our sins and purify us from all unrighteousness. I John 1:9 (NIV)

*

So overflowing is his kindness toward us that he took away all our sins through the blood of his Son, by whom we are saved. Ephesians 1:7 (TLB)

*

until I finally admitted all my sins to you and stopped trying to hide them. I said to myself, "I will confess them to the Lord." And you forgave me! All my guilt is gone. Psalm 32:5 (TLB)

Chapter 12

WHAT DID I LEARN?

G od stands with arms stretched wide open just waiting for us to repent and turn back to Him. It was the choices I made that made me feel rejected and alone. God never rejected me. When I became a Mormon, and when I started practicing witchcraft, seeking comfort in things other than Him, He did not stop loving me. He did not lower his outstretched arms.

It did not matter to God that I slept with different people, had several abortions, lied, cheated, or did drugs. None of that caused Him to lower His arms. When I reached the point in my life where I was tired of living without Him and decided that it was okay if I died, God did not lower His arms. Instead, He reached further for me, and I want you to know that God is reaching even further for you.

Listen to what the Lord says to you:

"There will be a few people along the way who will give you little nudges through the urging of the Holy Spirit.

You can expect that I will come upon people to push you and guide you in a specific direction. You can expect that through it all, it is my hand upon you."

I never thought I would have the kind of relationship that I now have with the Holy Spirit, and I never imagined I would be at peace mentally and free of medications. I sincerely seek to be in alignment with the Holy Spirit, and even though I don't claim to be perfect, my heartfelt desire is to live a life that is worthy of the sacrifice Jesus Christ made for me.

My deepest desire is that others experience the unspeakable joy that has replaced the desperation, despair, and loneliness which plagued me in the previous seasons of my life. Having experienced the darkest of nights in my life, I am a living witness that there is nothing too hard for God. It is the sincere love Christ has for each of us that manifests an amazing joy I want others to experience.

I am so thankful I found my way back to the love of my life, Jesus Christ. I found the love that makes me feel accepted, it makes me feel seen, and makes me feel like I belong.

Chapter 13

WHAT IS MY TRUTH?

There was something sexy and alluring about witchcraft. I liked the theatrics of it, and how it made me feel. When I was practicing it, I had a sense I could control my life and what happened to me. I liked being in control, and having the ability to do something most people around me couldn't do. That gave me a sense of value.

What I loved about my Mormon experience was seeing the commitment they exhibited toward their faith. Their sense of family and community captivated my heart from the moment I was introduced to it, because family and community gave me a sense of belonging. The Mormons stood firm on the teachings from the Book of Mormon and lived as it instructed them to. That kind of commitment to their beliefs was something I had not seen in my Christian community, nor had I experienced it as a follower of Jesus Christ.

I don't know if I was angry with God, or if I had just lost faith in Him because of the trauma I experienced in my childhood. I blamed Him for allowing me, as a child, to be hungry and forgotten. I was angry with my mother for being weak. I didn't understand her struggle.

I was angry with myself. Although I had those feelings about my mother and the Lord, I still loved them both and felt that it was wrong for me to feel that way.

I really didn't like working in the strip club. I didn't like the smell. I didn't like degrading myself in front of men for money. I thought that men were supposed to take care of women, but there was an arena where women were exploited for personal pleasure. I didn't like it.

In my relationships, I just wanted to be taken care of. I wanted to be valued and appreciated. I was tired of trying to figure it all out on my own.

I made decisions that made me feel separate from God. I isolated myself into a place of darkness, pain, turmoil, and loss, and I lived in physical agony because of it. My life seemed to be slipping away; like I was sliding so fast down the side of a hill coated in black greasy tar and I could not stop myself.

I never want to be in that place again; and I cannot imagine living without the Holy Spirit with me every day. So, whatever the cost, whatever the sacrifice, I am with the sovereign Lord until the end.

My advice to you is simply this--Taste and see that the Lord is good.

Prayer of Repentance

My Lord, You are the creator of all things. You know my end from my beginning, and You know the path I take. Father, Your throne is in Heaven and the earth is Your footstool. I thank You for allowing me to read the experiences shared in this book. It has caused me to look at my own life. My Lord, I repent for [*list out the actions, thoughts and feelings that cause you to fall short*].

Lord, I turn to You because Your Word commands that we come to You, all who are heavy laden, so we come to You and receive the rest You freely give. Your Word declares that Your yoke is easy, and Your burden is light. Lord, I lay down my burden because I am tired of carrying [*name the things that weigh you down*]. There is nothing I can do with it. Lord, You are the Master Surgeon. Search me and cut away anything that is not like You, then fill me with your Holy Spirit. Fill those empty places within me. Fill the wounded places with Your love; for apart from You, I am nothing.

Abba, I claim Jesus as my Lord and Savior. I submit myself to the Holy Spirit. Lord, let me live a life worthy of the sacrifice of Jesus Christ. Teach me Your way, and send Your divinely appointed people to support me on my journey. Speak plainly to me so that I may understand Your words and follow your instructions. Thank You for your grace, thank you for your mercy, and thank you for my advocate, the Holy Spirit.

In the name of Jesus,
Amen.

Ten Steps to Aid in Recovery from Witchcraft and the Occult

- **Daily Repentance.** Repent from that which is displeasing to God.

  Produce fruit in keeping with repentance. Matthew 3:8

- **Study the Word of God daily.** Out of the abundance of the heart the mouth speaks.

  You brood of vipers, how can you who are evil say anything good? For the mouth speaks what the heart is full of. Matthew 12:34

- **Spend time with Holy Spirit.**

  Behold, I stand at the door, and knock: if any man hear my voice, and open the door, I will come in to him, and will sup with him, and he with me. Revelation 3:20 (KJV)

- **Clean your home and all spaces of items from the occult.**
  25 The carved images of their gods you shall burn with fire. You shall not covet the silver or the gold that is on them or take it for yourselves, lest you be ensnared by it, for it is an abomination to the Lord your God. 26 And you shall not bring an abominable thing into your house and become devoted to destruction like it. You shall utterly detest and abhor it, for it is devoted to destruction. Deuteronomy 7:25-26 (ESV)

- **Deliverance.** Ask the Holy Spirit to reveal areas where you need deliverance.
  Submit yourselves, then, to God. Resist the devil, and he will flee from you. James 4:7

- **Assemble together with the saints.** Find a church home and support groups.
  Therefore, "Come out from them and be separate, says the Lord. "Touch no unclean thing, and I will receive you." 2 Corinthians 6:17

- **Discover what your spiritual gifts are and learn how to use them effectively. Remember, the enemy gives information that mimics the gifts of the Spirit.** Be sure to operate out of the *Holy* Spirit.
  Every good gift and every perfect gift is from above, and cometh down from the Father of lights, with whom is no

variableness, neither shadow of turning. James 1:17 (KJV)

- **Faith.** Have faith and trust the Holy Spirit in every area of your life.

  And without faith it is impossible to please him, for whoever would draw near to God must believe that he exists and that he rewards those who seek him. Hebrews 11:6 (ESV)

AUTHOR BIO

Kimberly C. Branch is an accomplished serial entrepreneur whose journey is marked by a deep commitment to putting God first. She has successfully launched and managed multiple ventures, demonstrating not only business acumen but also a passion for making a difference. Her ventures reflect her belief in the power of purpose-driven businesses to create lasting change in communities. A seasoned missionary with a heart for service, she has made positive impacts both here in the United States and in Ghana.

As a new author, Kimberly shares her experiences to inspire others. Her words are authentic and carry a message of empowerment and divine purpose. Kimberly C. Branch's story is a testament to the extraordinary impact that can be achieved when entrepreneurship, faith, and service converge. She continues to demonstrate that true success is not just measured in financial achievements but in the positive change one can bring to the world.

kimberly@kimberlycherie.com